LILY & LUCA'S ADV
ON AN
ISLAND TOUR

Lily & Luca's Adventure on an Island Tour

Published in Barbados by GABCEY Productions

ISBN 978-976-96534-4-3

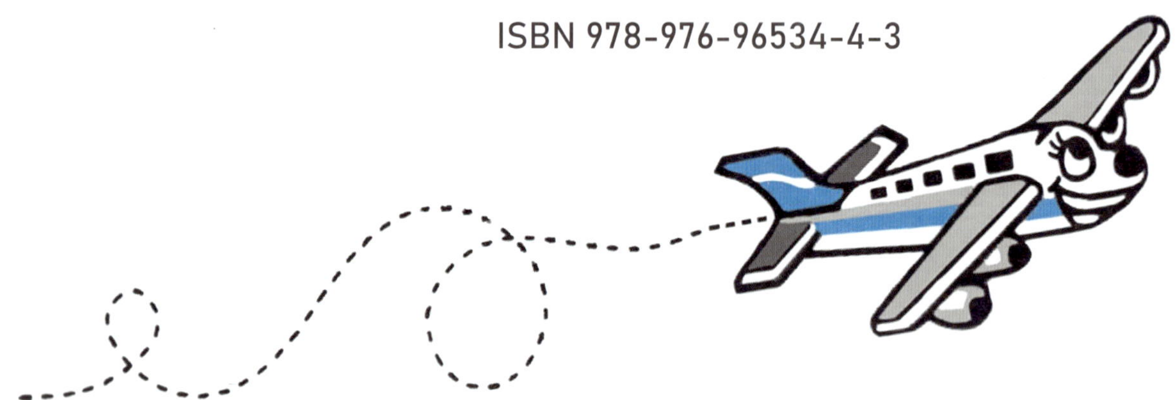

FUN ACTIVITIES TO DO

- Word Scramble
- Spelling Bee
- Colour by Numbers
- Word Search
- Spot the Difference
- Connect the Dots & Colour
- Secret Code
- Name the Location
- Crossword Challenge

1. **Bridgetown**
2. **Holetown**
3. **Speightstown**
4. **The Animal Flower Cave**
5. **St. Nicholas Abbey & Heritage Railway**
6. **Cherry Tree Hill**
7. **Morgan Lewis Windmill**
8. **Bathsheba**
9. **The Flower Forest Botanical Garden**
10. **Earthworks Pottery**
11. **Gun Hill**
12. **Marizayra Sanctuary**
13. **Oistins**

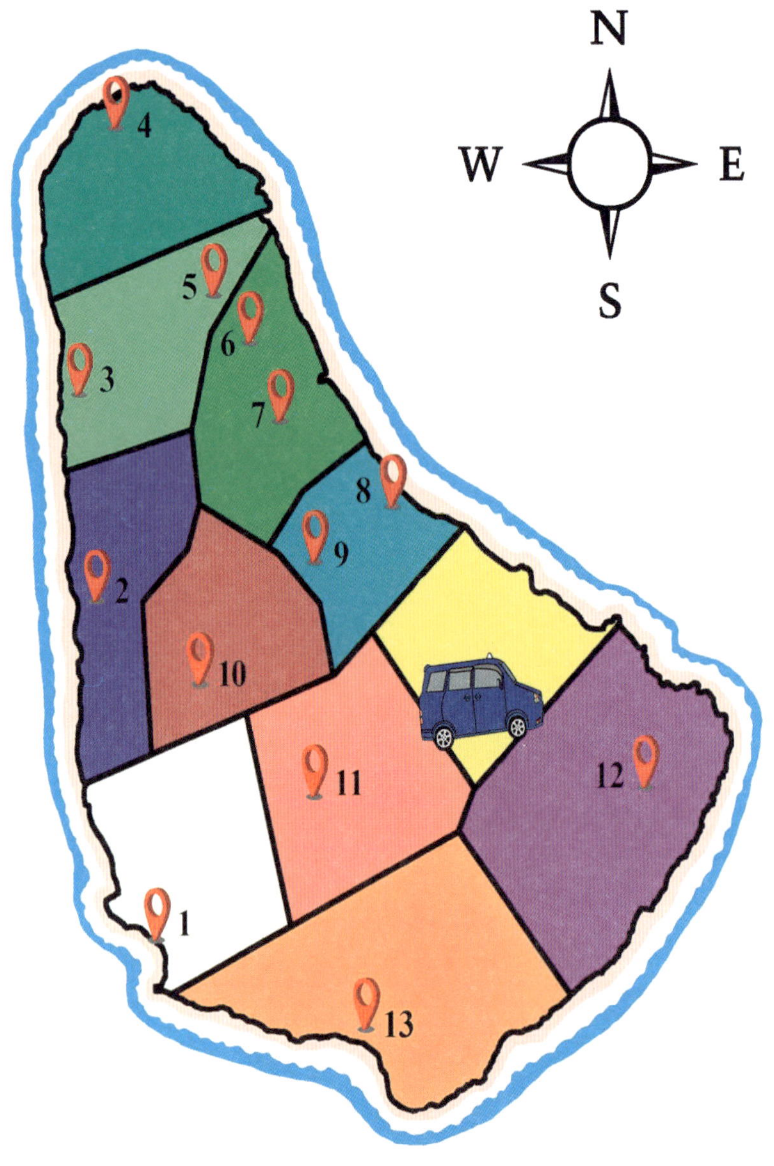

Lily and Luca love winter in Europe. They wear coats, scarves, boots and mittens to keep warm on the outside.

The siblings enjoy chasing each other with snow balls and making snowmen.

Without their knowledge, Lily and Luca's parents planned a very special family summer vacation.

ARRIVALS

The time to travel arrived.

Lily and Luca departed from England with their parents for the Caribbean island of Barbados.

After getting off the aeroplane, the family entered the airport arrivals hall and were welcomed with complimentary drinks by two friendly hostesses.

During their stay on the island the twins spent a lot of time with their grandparents who once lived in England.

Grandpa Pete taught Luca a popular game played throughout the Caribbean called 'Dominoes'.

Luca had fun matching the rectangular tiles and could not wait to teach his sister how to play the game.

On another occasion, they played softball cricket in the backyard while Mom and Grandma Rose prepared lunch.

Lily and Luca are members of a cricket club in their community of Yorkshire.

So, it was a delight to see a great display of their batting and bowling skills.

Lily bowled a softball and Luca hit it high in the air.

After their visit to the capital city of Bridgetown, the family was interested in seeing and exploring more of the island.

Dad called the friendly taxi operator 'Sweet Mouth' and booked an island tour.

Word Scramble

Unscramble the letters to make a word!

1.cktreic ___ ___ ___ ___ ___ ___ ___

2.wtse ___ ___ ___ ___

3.elngnad ___ ___ ___ ___ ___ ___ ___

4.hesosst ___ ___ ___ ___ ___ ___ ___

5.siph ___ ___ ___ ___

6.ctrasf ___ ___ ___ ___ ___ ___

7.ntarue ___ ___ ___ ___ ___ ___

8.crbibneaa ___ ___ ___ ___ ___ ___ ___ ___ ___

9.gdenar ___ ___ ___ ___ ___ ___

10.ecxusnior ___ ___ ___ ___ ___ ___ ___ ___ ___

'Sweet Mouth' collected the family at a meeting point in the capital city, Bridgetown where they boarded the van.

A young couple visiting from Brooklyn, New York also joined them on the tour.

They drove past the Bridgetown Port which handles both cargo vessels and cruise ships.

The visitors got a glimpse of a gigantic passenger cruise ship docked nearby.

Along the way, Lily and Luca peered through the window and were captivated by a small, colourful, wooden 'Chattel House'.

The word 'chattel' refers to the fact that this kind of property could be easily moved from one place to another.

These types of houses were popular after Emancipation and have a special place in Barbados' history.

The first stop was at a popular tour spot in Holetown on the west coast of the island.

Here they got a first-hand view of the historic St. James Parish Church which is one of the four oldest surviving churches in Barbados.

'Sweet Mouth' explained that the church was built near the landing site of the first English settlement in Barbados.

It was originally a wooden structure. However, after the impact of two hurricanes in 1675 and 1780 it was then rebuilt in stone.

The group drove into the parish of St. Peter and spent a short time walking through Speightstown.

Lily and Luca saw many historic buildings, retail shops and restaurants.

They also met local vendors along the road selling fruits, vegetables, arts and crafts.

Did you know?!

- Speightstown is located in the northern parish of St. Peter.
- Speightstown is the second largest town on the island.
- Speightstown was named after William Speight who owned the land the town was built on.
- Speightstown was one of the first ports to export tobacco, cotton, sugar and rum to England.
- Speightstown was named 'Little Bristol', because of its trading connections with the port of Bristol in England.
- Speightstown has many street vendors and shops.
- Speightstown is over 350 years old.

On their journey through the town, they stopped at a local bakery.

Lily and Luca saw a variety of popular pastries. Some they had never tasted before.

'Sweet Mouth' identified the currant slice, cassava pone, turnover, sweet bread and "lead pipe".

It was difficult for Lily and Luca to choose a pastry because they all looked so delicious.

Spelling Bee

Choose the correct spelling of each word and circle it!

1.	locule	locale	local
2.	cruise	cruse	cruisse
3.	vendar	vendor	vendorr
4.	chattle	chattel	chatell
5.	Brisstol	Bristal	Bristol
6.	view	vuew	veiw
7.	parishe	paresh	parish
8.	Spieghtstown	Speightstown	Spykestown

Next was a visit to North Point in St. Lucy.

The family toured a unique sea cave known as the Animal Flower Cave which got its name from the sea anemones that live in its pools.

The several openings looking out to the sea allowed them to enjoy the magnificent view of the ocean.

The island tour included a visit to the St. Nicholas Abbey and Heritage Steam Railway in the parish of St. Peter.

They were scheduled to explore the Railway and experience a historic tour of the Plantation House.

The island used to have a train service that ran from Bridgetown to Belleplaine in St. Andrew on the East Coast, between 1881 and 1938.

It provided a means of transport which made the island accessible to Barbadians of all walks of life.

Lily and Luca sat among other children in the steam engine train.

They quickly made friends with a boy named Shahmar who was excited to be part of the adventure.

Everyone, young and old, was thrilled to be on the scenic ride through the fields and wooded areas of the plantation.

Colour by Numbers

Use the key at the bottom of the page to colour in the picture of the train!

1 Yellow
2 Green
3 Blue
4 Red
5 Brown
6 Grey

After touring the Great House, a Jacobean style mansion, the children were shown a rare 1930s film of life on a sugar plantation.

They learnt how sugar cane was planted, harvested and processed into muscovado sugar which was placed into large barrels called 'hogsheads' and exported to England.

The British used sugar as a sweetener for their drinks such as tea and coffee.

From the Abbey they drove through a road lined with beautiful mahogany trees and stopped at Cherry Tree Hill.

The spot offers an excellent panoramic view of the eastern coastline of the island and of the Scotland District in St. Andrew.

Also in St. Andrew is the Morgan Lewis Windmill.

It is one of the oldest and longest-operating sugar mills in the Caribbean and once crushed sugar cane to produce juice which was used to make sugar.

The group strolled around the landscaped grounds of the historic mill.

Word Search

How many words can you find?

X	W	M	R	R	M	T	F	K	F	I	S	H	A	E
U	F	L	N	Z	S	Y	C	G	Z	Y	Z	X	P	L
F	U	L	E	A	T	P	O	T	T	E	R	Y	L	I
A	G	M	O	N	K	E	Y	P	D	R	R	I	I	F
G	D	C	D	R	R	P	N	S	I	U	M	T	G	G
B	C	V	L	B	A	D	M	E	E	D	X	F	H	E
A	P	P	E	G	S	U	G	P	N	S	T	X	T	K
K	L	F	W	N	C	A	Y	I	O	D	D	L	H	Y
E	S	P	H	X	T	C	W	D	J	D	N	O	O	J
R	B	O	E	I	P	U	L	D	N	Z	T	F	U	J
Y	I	N	R	T	O	H	R	A	Q	X	B	K	S	T
R	V	E	S	E	T	T	L	E	M	E	N	T	E	R
Y	H	M	R	T	W	S	L	Z	Q	L	O	G	I	A
Z	I	A	U	K	I	Q	C	X	K	O	D	Z	T	I
W	F	I	D	O	M	I	N	O	E	S	Q	P	N	N

ADVENTURE
BAKERY
COAST
DOMINOES
FISH
FLORA
HERITAGE
ISLAND
LIGHTHOUSE
MONKEY
PONE
POTTERY
SETTLEMENT
TRAIN
WINDMILL

At the easterly end of the island is beautiful Bathsheba in the parish of St. Joseph.

Lily and Luca saw spectacular views of breathtaking golden beaches and large rock formations.

Bathsheba's famous beach is known as 'The Soup Bowl' where surfing competitions also take place.

After enjoying the beauty of Bathsheba, the group ate lunch at one of the popular food shacks located in the area.

Everyone opted for 'Bajan' chicken soup which was the Special of the Day.

Lily and Luca liked the ground provisions and vegetables found in the soup, but they enjoyed the sweet dumplings most of all.

Next was an exploration of the unique Flower Forest Botanical Garden also in St. Joseph.

It is described as a peaceful, rainforest garden filled with attractive plants, flowers and palms.

Humming birds and several butterflies add to the natural beauty of the garden.

Lily easily recognized the Heliconia and Ginger Lily from among the lush flora.

Spot the Difference

Find 6 differences between the 2 pictures and circle them!

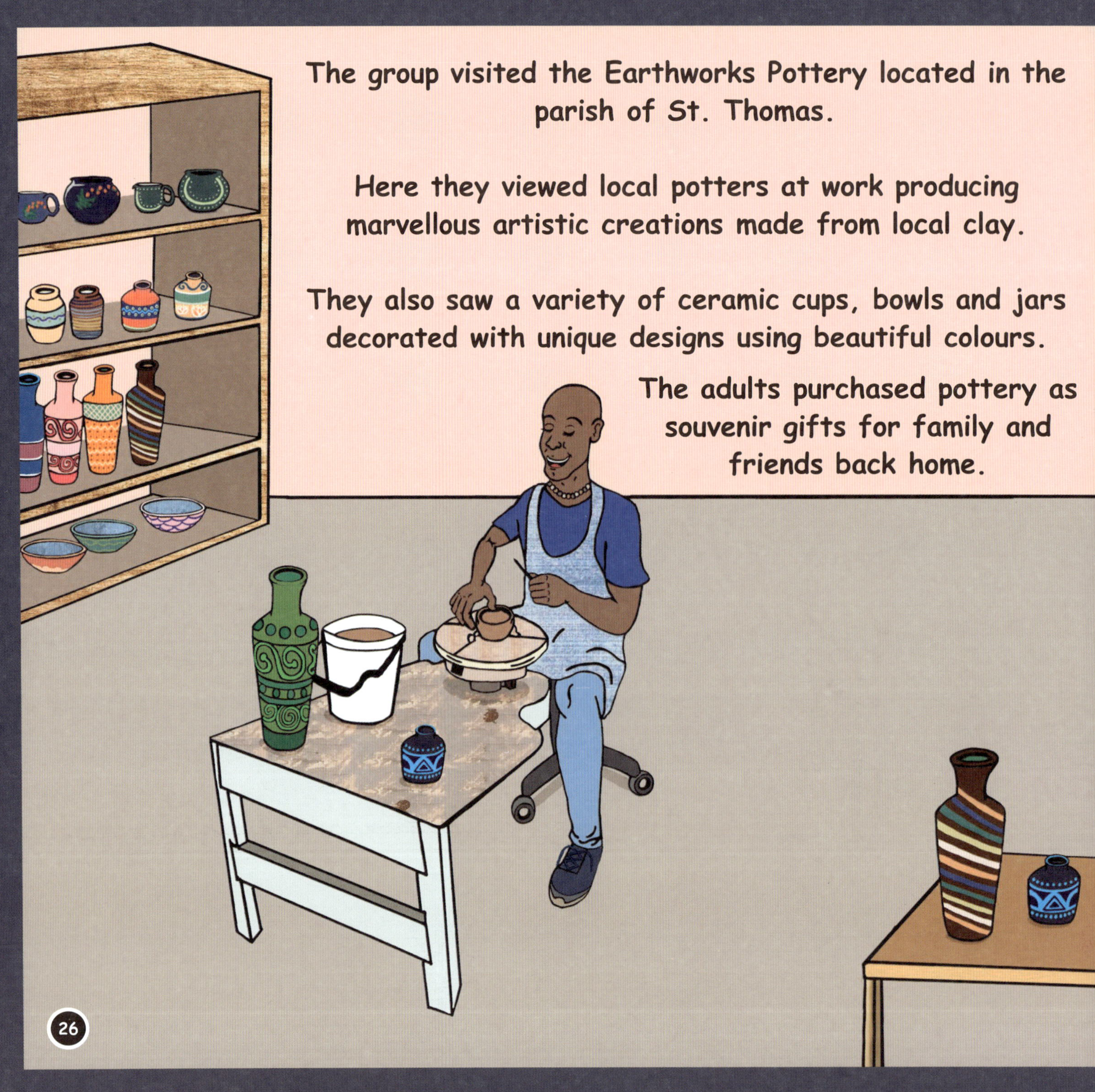

The group visited the Earthworks Pottery located in the parish of St. Thomas.

Here they viewed local potters at work producing marvellous artistic creations made from local clay.

They also saw a variety of ceramic cups, bowls and jars decorated with unique designs using beautiful colours.

The adults purchased pottery as souvenir gifts for family and friends back home.

The visitors were met by stunning gardens with flowers of every hue at Gun Hill in the parish of St. George.

The site is home to a Signal Station built in 1818.

It was the best of a chain of stations used to signal the arrival of cargo ships, the coming of enemy ships, and also to warn against slave uprisings on the island.

Cannons were positioned at Gun Hill to safeguard the island.

Not too far away was a huge, white stone statue of a lion.

Carved from coral rock by soldiers in 1868, the 'Lion at Gun Hill' is a beautiful work of art.

Lily and Luca got their parent's permission to capture a photo of them seated on the lion.

Connect the Dots & Colour

Connect the dots from numbers 1-50 to make a lion and then colour it!

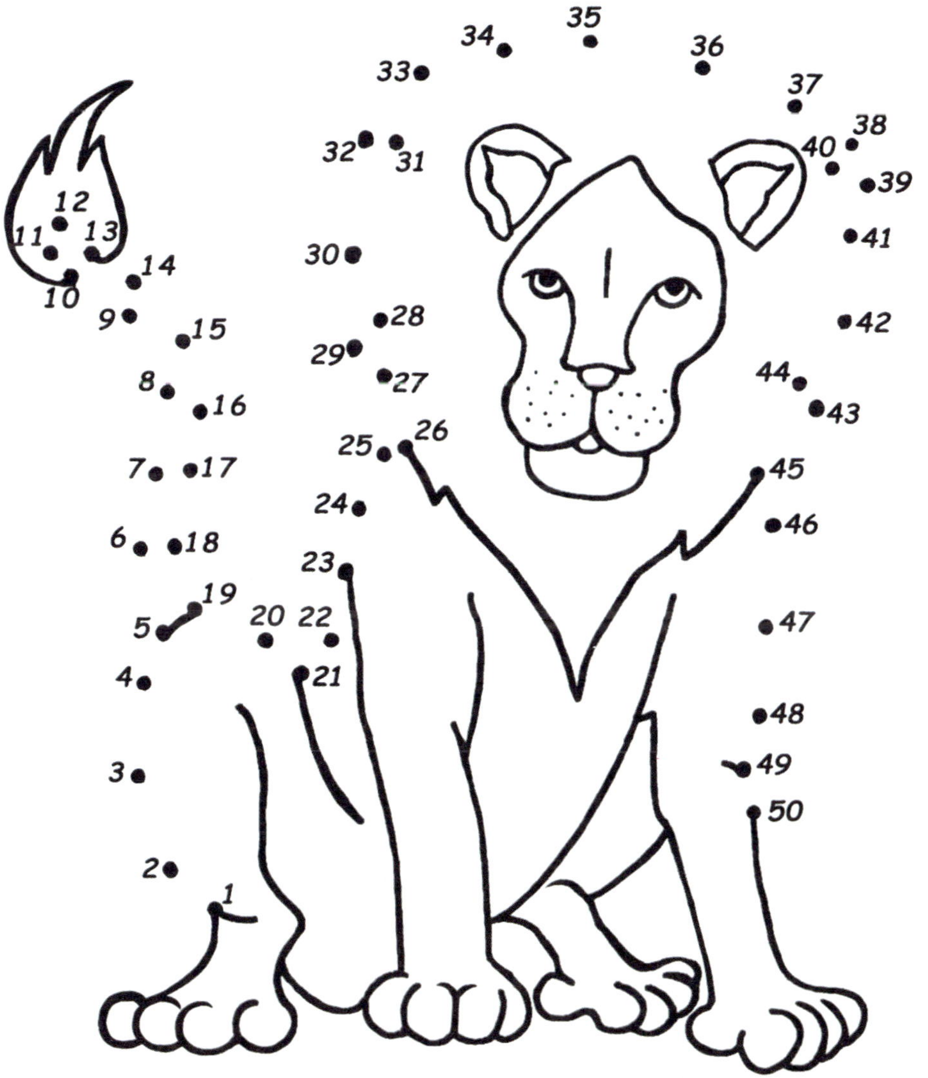

The sightseeing tour featured a drive through the parish of St. John where they enjoyed more panoramic views of amazing landscapes.

Soon after, they entered St. Philip for a visit at Marizayra Sanctuary to see nature at its finest.

Green monkeys, rabbits, ducks, snakes, lizards, tortoises, and several species of birds are some of the animals that children can interact with in this unique mini zoo.

The last stop on the exciting island tour was at the Oistins Fish Market in the southern parish of Christ Church.

Lily and Luca greeted a fisherman and in his hands was the biggest fish they had ever seen.

He told them it was a mahi-mahi which is locally referred to as 'Dolphin', and he encouraged them to come back and have it as a meal at the lively Friday night "fish-fry".

Name the Location

Use the image to name the correct site, place of interest or attraction!

1 

____

4 

____

2 

____

5 

____

3 

____

6 

____

Before saying their goodbyes, the family thanked 'Sweet Mouth' for the wonderful excursion around the beautiful island.

Lily and Luca were especially overjoyed about all the exciting things they got to see and experience in one day.

Secret Code

Lily and Luca left 'Sweet Mouth' a message in secret code, but he has no idea what it says. Can you help him out?

 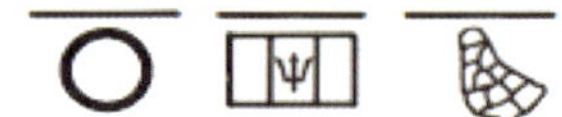

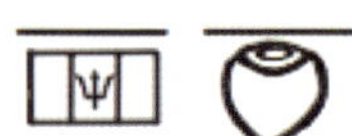  !

A	B	C	D	E	F	G	H	I	J	K	L	M

N	O	P	Q	R	S	T	U	V	W	X	Y	Z

Lily and Luca really enjoyed the adventure tour around Barbados.

The many historic sites, attractions and places of interest which they visited allowed them to learn more about the history and heritage of their second home.

While on a lovely outing organized by 'Peach Tree Picnics' they could not help, but think longingly about their next adventure.

Crossword Challenge

Fill the boxes with the answers that fit each clue!

ACROSS

5. A turtle that lives on land
6. A building used for public Christian worship
7. A place where cruise ships dock
9. A plant that grows in the Flower Forest (first word 'Ginger')
10. A group of people related by blood, marriage or adoption

DOWN

1. A large area of land where crops are grown
2. Something used to sweeten tea
3. Geographical location of The Animal Flower Cave
4. The study of the past
8. A material used to make pottery

1 2 3 4 5 6 7 8 9 10

We took pleasure in creating this illustrated book and would like to offer thanks to:

- God, for the ability to create and complete this book.

- Mrs. Margo Clarke and Ms. Sonja Welch, GCM, for taking the time to proof read our book.

- Pastor Noel Jordan Th.D., D.D., D. Min and Pastor Annette Jordan Th.D., D.D., D. Min, for their continual prayers and support.

- All persons who support local talent, which enables us to continue creating educational and enjoyable children's literature.

About the Authors

Gabriel and Stacey Welch are a married, Christian couple who have combined their artistic talents (artist & writer) to create the 'edutaining' Lily & Luca's Adventures® book series for children.

The Welchs at Hackleton's Cliff in St. John

Gabriel is the illustrator and also a visual artist. He was born and raised in Brussels, Belgium and has Barbadian heritage. Gabriel resides in Barbados and is happy to be able to use his talent to bring many elements of Barbados' history and Barbadian heritage alive.

Stacey is the co-author. She is a teacher by profession and has over ten years' experience in teaching. Stacey was born and raised in Barbados and enjoys creating children's literature which helps contribute to the development of education in Barbados.

The couple is on a mission to make reading more fun and enjoyable for children in Barbados and around the world. Their educational and entertaining story books aim to encourage children to read and learn new things while having fun.

To God be all the glory, honour and praise!

Contact Information

Email: gabceyproductions@gmail.com

Instagram: lily_luca_adventures

Facebook: Lily & Luca's Adventures

Answers to Worksheets

➢ Word Scramble

1. cricket
2. west
3. England
4. hostess
5. ship
6. crafts
7. nature
8. Caribbean
9. garden
10. excursion

➢ Spelling Bee

1. local
2. cruise
3. vendor
4. chattel
5. Bristol
6. view
7. parish
8, Speightstown

➢ Spot the Difference

1. Butterfly
2. Egg
3. Shoe
4. Leaf
5. Flower
6. Bird's wings

➢ Secret Code

THANK YOU FOR SHOWING US THE BEAUTY OF BARBADOS

➢ Name the Location

1. Bathsheba
2. Oistins
3. Gun Hill Signal Station
4. Marizayra Sanctuary
5. St. James Parish Church
6. Flower Forest Botanical Garden

➢ Crossword Challenge

Across 5. Tortoise 6. Church 7. Port 9. Lily 10. Family

Down 1. Plantation 2. Sugar 3. North 4. History 8. Clay